GW00630631

As Europe's top aviation museum. Duxford disp wartime aircraft that helped the Allies achieve including the Spitfire, Hurricane, Lancaster and B Duxford is also home to Europe's only example of (the type of aircraft that carried out the atomic bomb raids in Japan that brought the war in the Far East to an end.

The war on the ground is commemorated in Duxford's Land Warfare Exhibition Hall where tanks, military vehicles and artillery are presented in dramatic battlefield scenes which visitors can walk through. The most historic vehicles on display are the 'caravans' which carried Field Marshal Montgomery into war. The three lorries which comprised Monty's bedroom, private office and map room were his base for the latter part of the Second World War as the 21st Army Group advanced towards Germany. He was visited there by King George VI and also used the caravans for meetings with Winston Churchill and General Eisenhower. From these vehicles, his command centre, Montgomery went to accept the surrender of German forces in May 1945 on Luneberg Heath, bringing the war in Europe to a close.

Duxford itself is steeped in history. As a Battle of Britain fighter station and later an American 8th Air Force base, Duxford played a vital role in the Second World War. For more information about Duxford's past be sure to visit the History of Duxford Exhibition between Hangar 3 and the Control Tower.

If you have any comments regarding the interpreters please write to us at the following address:

Marketing Department, Imperial War Museum, Duxford Airfield, Cambridge CB2 4QR Tel: 01223 835000.

V FOR VICTORY

COMMEMORATING THE END OF THE SECOND WORLD WAR

1995 is the fiftieth anniversary of VE Day, VJ Day and the end of the Second World War and the Imperial War Museum Duxford is marking the occasion with a special "Living History" event called "V for Victory".

Each day until 3 September, costumed character interpreters in the roles of men and women from fifty years ago will interact with visitors and talk about their experiences during the Second World War. Subject to scheduling, you will have a chance to speak to a pilot, a submariner, a housewife, a tank driver and a female aircraft fitter.

They are here to bring Duxford's outstanding collection of Second World War aircraft and military vehicles to life and help you get the most from your visit by informing and entertaining you.

Please note that the interpreters will not all be here every day.

MEET THE INTERPRETERS

Flight Lieutenant Norman "Max" Miller DFM

This former Battle of Britain Spitfire pilot went on to fly Mosquitos around the D-Day period and hopes to become a test pilot after the war. He is based by the Mosquito in Hangar 1 or the Spitfire in Hangar 4.

Submariner John "Chats" Harris

After transferring from minesweepers in 1942 he transferred to Special Duties and served on midget submarines "Chats" lives up to his name and can tell you about the war beneath the waves. You will find him by the X-Craft exhibition in Hangar 3.

Womens Auxiliary Air Force Fitter Margaret Walker

Margaret joined up in 1941 out of patriotism, wanted a technical trade and was trained as a fitter. She can tell you about life as a WAAF and can be found by the Anson in Hangar 4 or the Lancaster in Hangar 2

Sergeant Patrick "Lofty" Connolly, Tank Commander

"Lofty" worked in the local steelworks in Scotland when war broke out but pressure from the lassies persuaded him to join up. After service in the Royal Engineers he became a Comet tank commander in the Fife and Forfar Yeomanry. "Lofty" will tell you about life in a tank during combat. You will find him by the Comet Tank in the Land Warfare Hall

Myrtle Butler, housewife

Myrtle is married and has two small boys. As she pegs out her washing she will be happy to share her thoughts about the war, rationing and her suspicions about the lady two doors up who gets more than her fair share from the butcher. Myrtle can be found in her prefab between Hangar 5 and the VI ramp.

FOREWORD

The Imperial War Museum was established by Act of Parliament in 1920. Its purpose is to collect, preserve and display material and information connected with military operations in which Britain, and the Commonwealth, have been involved since August 1914. Duxford Airfield is a department of the Imperial War Museum, very large and geographically distant from the headquarters in Lambeth Road, London, but nevertheless an integral part which is ideal for the display of large exhibits. Duxford is also the main storage site for archive film, photographs, books and documents – but this is in an area which is not normally open to visitors and those who wish to use these information sources should arrange access through Lambeth Road.

It is extremely appropriate for a section of the Imperial War Museum to be based at an historic fighter station such as Duxford. Duxford's service career spanned two World Wars. It played an important role in the Battle of Britain and was a fighter base for the men of the United States 8th Air Force for two and a half years. Much of the airfield is preserved as it was during the early 1940s.

Having sampled the collections at Duxford you may wish to visit one of the other parts of the Museum. HMS *Belfast*, moored in the Pool of London, is a museum ship which became part of the Imperial War Museum in 1978. The Cabinet War Rooms, off Whitehall, opened to the public in 1984 and is now one of London's major attractions.

The most spectacular developments have taken place in our headquarters in London. An ambitious rebuilding of the Museum within the walls of the original Bethlem Royal Hospital has resulted in a huge increase in gallery space, improved visitor facilities and dramatic new exhibitions including many items which have never before been on public display. I hope old friends and new will come along and share this exciting experience with us.

Alan Borg

Alan Borg
Director General
Imperial War Museum

The story of war in our century
Imperial War Museum · Lambeth Road · London SE1 6HZ
☎ 0171-416 5000

London's floating naval museum
HMS *Belfast*
Morgans Lane · Tooley Street · London SE1 2JH
☎ 0171-407 6434

The nerve centre of Britain's war effort
The Cabinet War Rooms
Clive Steps · King Charles Street · London SW1A 2AQ
☎ 0171-930 6961

Join the Friends and help support the Museum
Friends of the Imperial War Museum
Imperial War Museum · Lambeth Road · London SE1 6HZ ☎ 0171-416 5255

MUSEUM PLAN

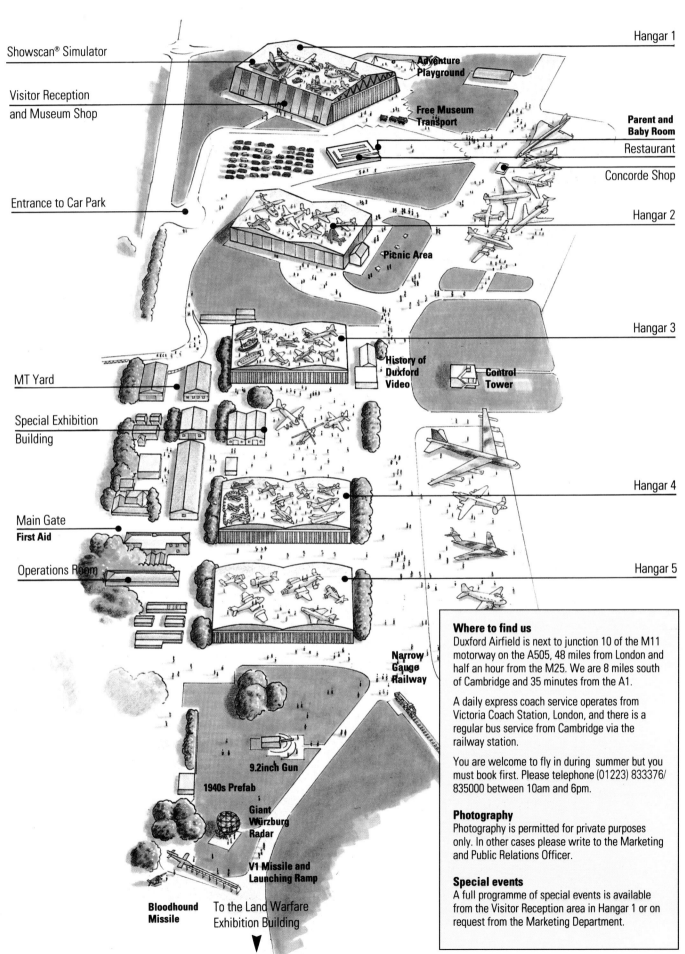

Showscan® Simulator

Visitor Reception and Museum Shop

Entrance to Car Park

MT Yard

Special Exhibition Building

Main Gate
First Aid

Operations Room

Hangar 1

Adventure Playground

Free Museum Transport

Parent and Baby Room

Restaurant

Concorde Shop

Hangar 2

Picnic Area

Hangar 3

History of Duxford Video

Control Tower

Hangar 4

Hangar 5

Narrow Gauge Railway

9.2inch Gun

1940s Prefab

Giant Würzburg Radar

V1 Missile and Launching Ramp

Bloodhound Missile

To the Land Warfare Exhibition Building
▼

Where to find us
Duxford Airfield is next to junction 10 of the M11 motorway on the A505, 48 miles from London and half an hour from the M25. We are 8 miles south of Cambridge and 35 minutes from the A1.

A daily express coach service operates from Victoria Coach Station, London, and there is a regular bus service from Cambridge via the railway station.

You are welcome to fly in during summer but you must book first. Please telephone (01223) 833376/835000 between 10am and 6pm.

Photography
Photography is permitted for private purposes only. In other cases please write to the Marketing and Public Relations Officer.

Special events
A full programme of special events is available from the Visitor Reception area in Hangar 1 or on request from the Marketing Department.

Thank you for buying this souvenir handbook. Its purpose is to help you get the most from your visit to Duxford Airfield and to explain something of why we are here, what we do and the philosophy of the Museum.

Our collections at Duxford include military aircraft and vehicles, tanks, guns and naval exhibits. The earliest examples date from the First World War and the most recent from the Gulf War. Our task is to preserve them for future generations, to explain what these exhibits did and their role in the history of

**Dr Alan Borg, Director
General of the Imperial
War Museum and Edward
Inman, Director of Duxford
Airfield, in Hangar 1.**
IWM

warfare in the twentieth century, and to present them in the best possible way to you, our visitors.

A major group of exhibits at Duxford is the collection of British civil airliners. These aircraft are owned and maintained by an organisation of dedicated volunteers called the Duxford Aviation Society. Its members contribute to the operation of Duxford in many ways but probably the most important is their help on restoration projects, putting in many hundreds of unpaid hours to preserve and enhance the collections. Their work, complementing that of the Museum's

professional staff, helps to make Duxford the largest centre of aircraft restoration in Europe. A popular feature is that most of our restoration projects are on public view.

Through our hugely successful partnership with the Cambridgeshire County Council, Duxford still has an operational runway, so we are able to stage flying displays and demonstrations. We are also able to attract the owners of important historic aircraft to base their collections at Duxford. Our visitors have the benefit of seeing these aircraft on display and frequently in flight. This all adds to Duxford's unique 'living' atmosphere.

Duxford is also the home of the finest collection of American military aircraft outside the United States, and our most ambitious future project is to house this collection in a special new building to be called 'The American Air Museum in Britain'.

The latest exhibition building at Duxford is the Land Warfare Hall. Purpose designed to house our tanks, military vehicles and artillery pieces, the Hall presents them in a dramatic and imaginative way.

The following chapters elaborate on some of these points and bring in other areas, for example our educational services, and the opportunities for commercial organisations both to benefit from facilities at Duxford and to contribute to the continued growth and success of the Museum.

Duxford receives nearly half a million visitors a year, which places us high on the list of public attractions outside London. We plan to extend and improve our exhibitions and facilities, and our priority is to offer the best possible service to our visitors.

Please feel free to ask questions of my staff here – they will do their best to give you the information you require. If you have a serious complaint about any aspect of the Museum I hope you will write to me direct. For without you Duxford would not be possible.

Edward Inman

**Edward Inman
Director
Duxford Airfield**

Opening Hours and Admission

Open every day except 1 January and 24–26 December. Summer (mid-March to mid-October) opening hours are 10.00am to 6.00pm, winter hours are 10.00am to 4.00pm.

Admission is charged. Reductions for senior citizens, disabled people, children aged 5–16, registered unemployed and students. Proof of status may be requested. Children under 5 are free. Party rates and a pre-booked educational group rate are normally available. Telephone Cambridge (01223) 835000 for details. No animals except guide dogs are allowed in the Museum.

HISTORY OF DUXFORD

The aerodrome at Duxford was built during the First World War and was one of the earliest Royal Air Force stations. Three of the original timber-trussed hangars survive (nos. 3, 4 and 5) and have been listed as buildings of special architectural and historic interest. There was a fourth hangar in the same style (the concrete base may still be seen between Hangars 3 and 4) but this was destroyed during the making of the film *The Battle of Britain* in 1968. A video presentation of the history of the airfield may be seen in the former Watch Office (the original 'control tower') next to Hangar 3.

During 1917 the Royal Flying Corps was carrying out an ambitious scheme to expand the service from around 160,000 to nearly 300,000 men. Duxford was one of a number of new stations constructed to train RFC aircrew.

Even before the construction of the airfield was finished Duxford became a temporary home to American airmen. In March 1918, some 200 members of the 159 and 137 United States Aero Squadrons began training at Duxford. Though there were local newspaper photographs of the American airmen taking part in sports events – notably on Independence Day, 4 July – they appear to have made little impression on wartime life in the area, and they returned to the United States almost immediately after the end of the First World War.

On 1 April 1918 the Royal Naval Air Service and the Royal Flying Corps were merged and became the Royal Air Force, the world's first fully independent air force. By August 1918 the airfield was completed and also became part of the newly formed service. After the war ended on 11 November 1918 it was used as a base for the disbandment of squadrons from the Continent.

At this time the RAF had 188 operational squadrons and 291,000 officers and men. Peacetime commitments required a much smaller force. By 1920 the RAF was reduced to 12 squadrons and 31,500 officers and men and the future of RAF Duxford was in grave doubt. Later that year Emile Mond, whose pilot son had been killed in the First World War, offered to endow a Chair of Aeronautical Engineering at Cambridge University provided the RAF made facilities for research in flight available nearby. Duxford was chosen for this role and remained open. Over the years Duxford was destined to maintain close scientific links with the university.

▼ **Members of the United States Aero Squadrons celebrate Independence Day in Cambridge, 4 July 1918.**
Reproduced by permission of the Syndics of Cambridge University Library.

A Glorious "Fourth."

Chronicle Photos.]
Independence Day was celebrated in Cambridge by a large number of American troops, who assembled the town early in the morning and spent a right royal day. (1) The baseball match on Fenner's. The striker has just hit the ball (which can be seen travelling at a great pace out of the diamond). (2) The winning baseball team from Duxford. (3) The American Flag flying over the Great Eastern Station, Cambridge, a welcome to all Americans coming into the town. (4) After the game at Fenner's, Col. Edwards calls for cheers for the Union Jack and Stars and Stripes, which were given in real American fashion.

▼ **A 1921 souvenir postcard of No.2 Flying Training School, RAF.**
IWM Neg. No. HU39316

◄ **Duxford Airfield from the air in 1918, looking east.**
IWM Neg. No. Q96065

4

RAF Duxford became No.2 Flying Training School in April 1920, and was equipped with Avro 504s, Bristol Fighters and DH9As. In 1923 limited expansion of the RAF meant that a training flight of Sopwith Snipes was added to the Flying Training School. From the pilots and aircraft at Duxford the nuclei of three fighter

1935 was King George V's Silver Jubilee year and the King took the salute at Duxford on Saturday 6 July as 20 squadrons of the RAF flew past in review order. More than 100,000 members of the public came to see the spectacle.

In 1936 Flight Lieutenant (later Air Commodore Sir) Frank Whittle was studying at Cambridge University and flew regularly from Duxford as a member of the Cambridge University Air Squadron. Whittle was the first person to think of using a jet turbine as a means of powering an aircraft and his engineering genius enabled Britain to produce the jet-powered Gloster Meteor in 1943 – the Allies' first operational jet fighter.

By the summer of 1938 No.19 Squadron's reputation was such that it was chosen to be the first RAF squadron to re-equip with the new Spitfire and the first Spitfire was flown into Duxford on 4 August 1938 by Jeffrey Quill, Supermarine's test pilot. The Gauntlet was by this time outdated but it was with this aircraft

No.19 Squadron Gauntlets in 1935.
IWM Neg. No. HU41581

Heyford bombers fly over Duxford as part of King George V's Silver Jubilee Review of the Royal Air Force, 6 July 1935.
IWM Neg. No. HU41577

Inset: **Gloster Grebes of No.19 Squadron in one of the Duxford hangars in 1927.**
IWM Neg. No. Q102726

squadrons were formed, Nos.19, 29 and 111. In 1924 No.2 Flying Training School left and Duxford became a fighter station, a role it was to carry out with distinction for 37 years.

By the beginning of 1925 Duxford's three fighter squadrons were up to strength with Gloster Grebes and Armstrong Whitworth Siskins. No.19 Squadron re-equipped with Bristol Bulldogs in 1931 and, at the beginning of 1935, was chosen as the first squadron to fly the RAF's fastest new fighter, the 230 mph Gloster Gauntlet.

that 19 and 66 Squadrons stood by at Duxford during the Munich crisis of September/October 1938, for re-equipment with Spitfires was not completed until the end of that year. On 3 September 1939 Britain declared war on Germany.

In February 1940 one of the heroes of the Second World War was posted to No.19 Squadron at Duxford. Flying Officer Douglas Bader had lost both his legs in an air crash several years earlier and had been discharged from the RAF as permanently unfit while undertaking ground duties at Duxford in 1933. Desperate to serve his country in the way he knew best, he badgered the RAF until he was allowed to rejoin. He would not permit his artificial limbs to deter him and soon showed himself to be a courageous pilot and fine leader of men.

By June 1940 Belgium, Holland and France had fallen to the German forces and the conquest of Britain was their next objective. Once the threat was realised Duxford was placed in a high state of readiness. To create space for additional units at Duxford, 19 Squadron moved to nearby Fowlmere, another First World War airfield which had closed in 1922 but was reactivated in 1940.

June 1940 saw the start of Hitler's attempt to dominate the skies over Britain as a prelude to invasion. The period of intensive air fighting that followed has become known as the Battle of Britain.

Duxford's first Hurricanes arrived in July with the formation of No.310 Squadron made up of Czech pilots who had escaped from France. At the end of August the Commander in Chief of 12 Group, Air Vice-Marshal Trafford Leigh-Mallory, ordered the Hurricanes of 242 Squadron, now commanded by Douglas Bader, down from Coltishall to join 19 and 310 Squadrons on daily standby at Duxford.

Leigh-Mallory was impressed with the performance of 19 and 310 Squadrons and authorised Bader to lead 242, 19 and 310 as a Wing. By this time the Luftwaffe had turned their attention to London. On 9 September the Duxford squadrons claimed to have destroyed twenty of the enemy for the loss of four Hurricanes and two pilots. On the strength of this two more squadrons were added to the Wing, No.302 (Polish) with Hurricanes, and the Spitfires of No.611 Auxiliary which had mobilised at Duxford a year before. Every day some sixty Spitfires and Hurricanes were dispersed around Duxford and Fowlmere. Bader's 'Big Wing', now known more formally

▼ A formation of six No. Squadron Spitfires in October 1938.
IWM Neg. No. CH21

▲ Squadron Leader Douglas Bader with a 242 Squadron Hurricane, 26 September 1940.
IWM Neg. No. CH1405

◀ A 1940 aerial photograph of Duxford taken by the Luftwaffe. Cambridge is actually in the opposite direction to that shown on the photograph.
IWM Neg. No. MH26526

▲ Spitfire Press Day at Duxford, 4 May 1939.
IWM Neg. No. HU27846

GB 1069 bc   Maßstab etwa 1:17 000   Duxford Fliegerhorst

G B 1069 bc
Geheim

Kriegsaufnahme: 0918
Nachträge: 7.9.40

Karte: 1:100 000
Blatt 24

Länge (ostw. Greenw.): 0°08'
Nördl. Breite: 52°05'

Zielhöhe über N N 29 m

G.B. 10 69   Fliegerhorst
1) 3 Flugzeughallen
2) 1 Flugzeughalle, zerstört
3) Unterkunftsgebäude, zerstört
4) Splittersichere Abstellplätze f.Flugzeuge
5) Flakstellungen
6) Kläranlage
7) Scheinwerferstellung

Lft. Kdo. 2,

as 12 Group Wing, was ready for action by 15 September 1940, which became known as 'Battle of Britain Day'. On this historic day they took to the air twice against Luftwaffe attacks and by the evening claimed to have destroyed 42 enemy aircraft.

After the Battle of Britain Duxford also became the home of several specialist units, among them the Air Fighting Development Unit. The AFDU's equipment included captured German aircraft, restored to flying condition for evaluation. The sight of a Messerschmitt 109, Junkers 88 or Heinkel 111 around Duxford at that time did not necessarily have the local people running for cover.

Squadrons with newly-acquired aircraft were posted to Duxford for trials. One of these was No.601 Squadron, the only RAF squadron to be equipped with the unusual American Bell Airacobra. Duxford also played a major part in developing the Hawker Typhoon into a formidable low-level and ground attack fighter

In October 1942, a squadron of the United States 350th Fighter Group arrived at Duxford. The group, equipped with Bell Airacobras, did not see operational service from England but moved on to join the US 12th Air Force in North Africa.

In April 1943 the airfield was fully handed over to the United States 8th Air Force, which had begun to arrive in Britain the previous May. The 8th was the largest of the United

and in 1942 the first Typhoon Wing was formed here. The first Wing operation – an offensive sweep over Northern France – took place on 20 June 1942. One of those who participated was Duxford's then station commander, Group Captain John Grandy, now Marshal of the Royal Air Force Sir John Grandy and Chairman of the Trustees of the Imperial War Museum from 1978 to 1989.

States Army Air Forces at this time, in the order of 200,000 men at its peak strength. Duxford now became Base 357 and the headquarters of the 78th Fighter Group, who were officially welcomed when King George VI and Queen Elizabeth visited the airfield on 26 May 1943.

The 78th FG flew P-47 Thunderbolts and acted as fighter escort to the large US bomber raids in occupied Europe and Germany itself. They also undertook sweeps over hostile territory and became adept at strafing, flying in at very low level to destroy ground installations and small targets. Captain Charles London of the 83rd Fighter Squadron at Duxford became the first official 8th Air Force Ace.

On D-Day, 6 June 1944, the long-awaited beginning of the Allied invasion of occupied Europe, every available 78th Fighter Group Thunderbolt was giving air cover to the Allied invasion fleet as it crossed the Channel. Later the group took part in raids on railway targets ahead of the ground forces and during the airborne landings at Arnhem in the Netherlands the 78th were awarded a Distinguished Unit Citation for the number of sorties carried out. The 78th also distinguished themselves by shooting down the first Me262 jet aircraft claimed by the 8th Air Force, and by the end of the war were credited with the destruction of 697 enemy aircraft either in the air or on the ground. The station was officially handed back to the Royal Air Force on 1 December 1945.

During their stay the Americans had laid a perforated steel plate runway over the grass strip and it was deemed adequate by the RAF for jet aircraft in the short term. The first aircraft to return to Duxford were Spitfires but by 1947 they were gone, replaced by Gloster

▼ Aerial view of Duxford.
IWM Neg. No. DUX(T)88/42/40

Meteors. By 1951 a new concrete runway had been laid and a type T2 hangar erected alongside the four First World War hangars. Although the original T2 hangar has gone the Museum has since erected another Second World War T2 hangar on the same site (Hangar 2). No.65 Squadron were then operating Meteors, later converting to Hawker Hunters. In September 1958 No.64 Squadron took on the last type of fighter to serve with the RAF at Duxford – the Gloster Javelin FAW 7.

The station was entering its last operational phase, for the defence needs which had called Duxford into being as a fighter station no longer applied. Duxford was too far south and too far inland, and the costly improvements required for supersonic fighters could not be justified. In July 1961 the last operational RAF flight was made from Duxford and for some 15 years the future of the airfield remained in the balance.

The Ministry of Defence declared its intention to dispose of the airfield in 1969. Plans for a regional sports centre and a prison were put forward but eventually came to nothing. The Imperial War Museum had been looking for a suitable site for the storage, restoration and eventual display of exhibits too large for its headquarters in Lambeth Road, London, and obtained permission to use the airfield for this purpose. Cambridgeshire County Council bought the runway in 1977 and joined with the Imperial War Museum and the Duxford Aviation Society to give this once abandoned aerodrome a whole new lease of life.

NOT TO BE MISSED...

The *Jesse Lumb* lifeboat was built in 1939 with a legacy of £9,000 bequeathed by Miss A Lumb whose family owned a high quality textile works in Huddersfield, West Yorkshire. A condition of the legacy was that the boat should be named after her brother, Jesse.

During the Second World War the *Jesse Lumb* was stationed at Bembridge, Isle of Wight, and rescued crews of aircraft shot down during the Battle of Britain, and of vessels in distress due to enemy action and storms. Later, in 1968, still in the same waters, she stood by HM Submarine *Alliance* which was stranded on the rocks of the Bembridge Ledge and from which 38 men were winched to safety by RAF helicopters.

Jesse Lumb was the last wartime lifeboat of this type in service with the Royal National Lifeboat Institution. She was moved to Duxford for display in 1980.

IWM Neg. No. DUX90/28/9

Jesse Lumb is located in Hangar 3.

SEVENTY YEARS OF BRITISH MILITARY AVIATION ON DISPLAY

For most of aviation's short history, Britain has played a major role in the field of military aircraft design and construction. This tradition of achievement and innovation can be seen throughout the collection of Royal Flying Corps, Royal Air Force and Royal Navy aircraft at Duxford.

The *Dawn Patrol* exhibition in Hangar 4 features two extremely rare and important aircraft from the First World War (1914–1918). The **Royal Aircraft Factory RE8** – RE stood for Reconnaissance Experimental – was introduced into Royal Flying Corps service in

1918. Although over 4,000 RE8s were built between 1916 and 1918, Duxford's example is one of only two complete RE8s to have survived.

The combat debut of the two-seat **Bristol Fighter** was disastrous, four out of six aircraft being shot down on their first patrol in April 1917. The RFC crews had used the standard two-seater tactic of leaving the observer to defend the aircraft. When the British pilots began to fly the aircraft as if it were a single-seat fighter and used the forward-firing Vickers gun to full effect, the 'Brisfit' became extremely effective and went on to equip all RFC fighter-reconnaissance squadrons. When production of the Bristol Fighter ceased in 1927 more than 5,250 had been built and in the post-war role of army co-operation the type served in Britain and overseas until 1932.

In 1934 the Avro 652 monoplane airliner entered service with Imperial Airways. From this design stemmed the **Avro Anson** which

◀ Two Anson Mark 1s of No.217 Squadron on coastal reconnaissance in France during 1940.
IWM Neg. No. C2118

▲ The Museum's RE8, F3556.
IWM

1916 and became one of the most widely used reconnaissance and artillery-spotting aircraft of the war. Although extremely stable in flight the RE8's poor manoeuvrability and low speed made it a prime target for enemy fighters. Despite these defects the RE8 equipped 19 squadrons on the Western Front by October

▶ A Bristol Fighter features in the *Dawn Patrol* Exhibition in Hangar 4.
Reeve Photography

went into RAF service in February 1936 as a light bomber and served in various roles up to 1968. The Anson was the RAF's first monoplane and its first aircraft with a retractable undercarriage. When the Second World War (1939–1945) broke out, the Anson went into action as a bomber with Coastal Command and on 5 September 1939 made the first RAF attack of the war on a German submarine.

Duxford's collection of wartime training aircraft includes a **Miles Magister** elementary trainer, dating from 1937, and an **Airspeed Oxford** twin engined trainer, a type mainly used to train Bomber Command crews.

One of Duxford's more unusual exhibits is the **Cierva Autogiro**, a civilian-designed aircraft taken over by the RAF and used for radar calibration during the war. Unlike a

helicopter the autogiro's rotor is kept in motion by the forward speed of the aircraft, which gives lift but not the capacity to hover.

The most famous and successful British heavy bomber used by the RAF during the Second World War was the **Avro Lancaster**. The Lancaster was the last of the four-engined heavy bombers to enter RAF service in wartime. Developed from the failed twin-engined Manchester bomber, Lancasters were delivered to Bomber Command in early 1942 and first flew into action on 17 April 1942. Lancasters took part in every major night attack on Germany and by May 1945 a total of 61 RAF squadrons were equipped with the type. One of the most famous Lancaster operations was the 'Dam Busters' raid in May

1943 which destroyed the Möhne and Eder dams. Production of Lancasters ceased in 1946 when 7,366 had been built.

The **de Havilland Mosquito** was the fastest and most versatile light bomber of the Second World War. The 'Wooden Wonder', as the Mosquito was nicknamed, was first used operationally in May 1942 and proved equally effective as a bomber, night fighter, ground attack and photographic reconnaissance aircraft. Duxford's Mosquito is a B35, the last bomber version built, which was replaced in service by the jet-engined **Canberra** in 1953.

During the Second World War the Royal Navy Fleet Air Arm also played a vital role in the Allied victory. Duxford has two wartime Royal Navy aircraft on display.

The **Fairey Swordfish** was such a successful design that, despite its antiquated appearance, it outclassed the aircraft intended to replace it and served throughout the Second World War. The 'Stringbag' entered Fleet Air Arm service in 1936 and served principally as a torpedo carrier and spotter-reconnaissance aircraft until 1945. The most successful Swordfish sortie was the attack on the Italian naval base at Taranto on 10–11 November 1940 when 21 Swordfish destroyed three battleships, a cruiser, two destroyers and other warships. Total Swordfish production reached 2,391.

When the **Fairey Firefly** entered service in July 1943 it became the Royal Navy's main carrier-borne fighter-reconnaissance aircraft. The Firefly's notable feats include the part it played in the attacks against the German

battleship *Tirpitz*, and on Japanese oil refineries in Sumatra during January 1945.

Probably the most famous fighter aircraft of all time, the **Supermarine Spitfire** entered RAF service at Duxford in 1938. When production ceased in 1949 more than 22,000 Spitfires and Seafires (Spitfires adapted for use on aircraft carriers) had been built.

The Second World War hastened the development of an entirely new means of aircraft propulsion, the jet engine. In 1944 Allied aircrew began to encounter a new high-speed swept wing aircraft in the skies over Germany – the Messerschmitt Me262. This revolutionary high-performance aircraft was powered by jet engines and, had it been produced earlier in greater numbers, could have restored command of the skies over Germany to the Luftwaffe.

Equally alarming for Allied aircrew was the appearance in the same year of the **Messerschmitt Me163 Komet** which was perhaps the most futuristic aircraft of the war. However, this rocket-powered interceptor suffered from short flight endurance and the use of unstable fuels led to numerous accidents during the Komet's unconventional skid-landings.

The Me262 was not the only wartime jet. Britain's **Gloster Meteor**, which first took to the air in March 1943, was the only operational Allied jet fighter during the war. From 1950 to 1955 the **Meteor F8** was the RAF's principal day fighter and was produced in greater numbers than any other version. Nos.64 and 65 Squadrons stationed at Duxford were both equipped with the F8 in the early 1950s.

In 1946 the **de Havilland Vampire**

became the second jet fighter to enter RAF service. Originally an interceptor, Vampire variants also served as fighter-bombers, night fighters, and trainers. The **Vampire T11** on display at Duxford is an example of the standard advanced jet trainer which equipped the service until the late 1960s.

From July 1954 the **Hawker Hunter** replaced the Meteor F8 as the main front line interceptor. The Hunter's versatility and excellent handling characteristics made it the outstanding British post-war fighter and ensured its great export success. Of the 2,000 Hunters built, over 1,100 were eventually sold abroad and served with 20 foreign air forces. The **Hunter F6** on display flew from Duxford with No.65 Squadron in 1956 and 1957.

The **Gloster Javelin**, the world's first twin-jet delta-wing fighter was the RAF's main

Douglas C-47 Skytrain in United States service) was used in large numbers by the RAF from 1942 to 1950. It was developed from the DC-3, the most widely used airliner of all time. It owed its success to its toughness, power and stability and in all over 10,000 were built. From 1948 the **Handley Page Hastings** replaced the **Avro York** as the standard long-range transport of RAF Transport Command. The Hastings played a

◀ Hastings TG 528 served with Nos.24 and 36 Squadrons of RAF Transport Command in the United Kingdom, Kenya, Suez and Cyprus.
▼ Since coming to Duxford in 1979 the aircraft has been fully restored both internally and externally.
IWM Neg. No. DXP(T) 87/18/8
Reeve Photography

▼ Pilots, navigators and ground crews of No.64 Squadron with their Javelin Mk7s at RAF Duxford in May 1959.
WM Neg. No. HU46502

▶ This aircraft, XM 135, was the second production Lightning. It served with the Air Fighting Development Unit at RAF Coltishall for three years before joining No.74 Squadron until 1964. During this period it flew in the Fighter Command Aerobatic Team. It then served as a supersonic target aircraft until 1971. After a period at No.60 Maintenance Unit, RAF Leconfield, XM 135 was flown to Duxford in November 1974 to join the Imperial War Museum collection.
Reeve Photography

night fighter from 1956 to 1964. Designed to operate at high altitudes and in all weathers, night or day, Javelins equipped No.64 Squadron at Duxford in the final years of the station's operational life from 1958 to 1961.

The **English Electric Lightning** which entered service in 1960 was the RAF's first supersonic fighter and the first aircraft to exceed the speed of sound in level flight over Britain. The Lightning could fly at twice the speed of the Hunter which it replaced in RAF service and could climb at a rate of 50,000ft (15,240m) per minute. This extremely high performance interceptor remained in front line use with RAF Strike Command until 1988.

The importance of military transport aircraft is often under-estimated but their role is vital. The **Dakota** (known as the

major role in the Berlin Airlift of 1949. Although initially designed as a transport aircraft, some Hastings were converted for meteorological reconnaissance duties with RAF Coastal Command and others for use as trainers for Bomber Command. From 1954 the larger and faster **Bristol Britannia** took over the long-range strategic transport role of the Hastings.

During and after the Second World War RAF Coastal Command used modified heavy bombers such as the Lancaster for maritime reconnaissance duties. The **Avro Shackleton**, developed from the Lancaster and Lincoln, continued this tradition. The first

Shackletons equipped Coastal Command from 1951 and the MR3 version on display at Duxford served into the 1970s until replaced by the Nimrod. Shackletons continued to serve in the Airborne Early Warning (AEW) role into the late 1980s.

The Royal Navy **Fairey Gannet** also served in the AEW role, operating from aircraft carriers between 1960 and the early 1970s. The other principal variant of the Gannet

bomber. It entered service in 1951 and the Canberra's advanced design made it a record breaker. Canberras were used in action over Malaya and during the Suez crisis of 1956. They went on to be widely exported and manufactured under licence in the United States, as the Martin B-57. Variants were also used for training, target-towing and photographic reconnaissance.

From the mid 1950s until 1969 the **Avro**

▼ By the time Shackleton XF 708 flew into Duxford in August 1972 it had flown over 6,500 hours and made almost 2,500 landings.
Reeve Photography

▶ The Museum's Gannet XG 797 on the flight deck of HMS *Centaur* in 1960 while serving with No.870 Squadron Fleet Air Arm.
IWM Neg. No. HU43089

▶ Vulcan B2 of No.44 Squadron.
British Aerospace

operated in the anti-submarine role from 1955 to the late 1960s and Duxford's Gannet is an example of this type.

The **English Electric Canberra** was the first British jet bomber and was designed as a high-speed replacement for the Avro Lincoln

Vulcan, **Handley Page Victor** and the Vickers Valiant made up RAF Bomber Command's 'V'-Bomber Force, Britain's airborne nuclear deterrent. From 1958, 'V'-Bomber bases were defended by **Bloodhound** surface-to-air missiles. The Vulcan, the first four-engined aircraft to use the delta wing, entered RAF service in 1957 and served as a nuclear weapon platform for almost all of its service life. Initially armed only with free-fall nuclear bombs, from 1963 the Vulcan also carried the **Blue Steel** stand-off missile. The Vulcan went to war in 1982, when it used conventional weapons against Argentinian positions on the Falkland Islands. The Vulcan was withdrawn from service in 1984, replaced by the Tornado.

▲ English Electric Canberra B6s.
IWM Neg. No. C(AM)1688

▲ Duxford's Vulcan B2, XJ 824, first joined No.27 Squadron at Scampton in May 1961. In an operational life of twenty years it saw service with a number of different RAF units in the United Kingdom and Cyprus, ending its career with No.101 Squadron at Waddington in 1981. XJ 824 made its final flight, to Duxford, in March 1982.
Jarrold

Designed initially as a replacement for the Canberra the **British Aircraft Corporation TSR-2** developed into a potential replacement for the RAF 'V'-bombers. However, in 1965 the government decided that the estimated costs of research, development and production of

the TSR-2 would be prohibitive, and cancelled the project.

The Victor was the last of the 'V'-bombers to enter RAF service in 1958. Also equipped with the Blue Steel missile, the Victor retained a nuclear capability until 1975. A number of these aircraft, including the example on display at Duxford, were converted into

tankers for in-flight refuelling with fuel tanks mounted in the bomb-bay. The RAF's Victors continued in this role into the 1990s and served in the combat zone during the Gulf War.

▼ A Royal Air Force Victor K2 tanker.
RAF

A total of 61,000lb (27,500kg) of thrust is developed by the two Olympus engines of the TSR-2 as it takes off from Boscombe Down for a test flight in 1964.
British Aerospace

NOT TO BE MISSED...

Giant Würzburg radar units were used for fighter-control in the German defensive system against the Allied bombing offensive from 1942 until the end of the Second World War. They were operated in pairs, one being used to track a target bomber and the second controlling a defending fighter. At least 1,500 examples of the Giant Würzburg were built.

The principle of 'seeing' by bouncing radio waves off an object was first proposed by a German scientist in 1904. Research and development in radar (or radio detection finding as it was called until 1944) proceeded in parallel in Britain and Germany in the 1930s.

Telefunken began the production of the Small Würzburg gun-laying and ground control radar, with a range of 25 miles, during 1938. The success of the small short-range equipment led to the development of the Giant Würzburg which had (in ideal conditions) a range of up to 50 miles.

Duxford's example of the Giant Würzburg radar was brought by the late Professor

Sir Martin Ryle FRS from Germany after the Second World War. In 1959 it was erected at the Mullard Radio Astronomy Laboratory at Lord's Bridge near Cambridge, and was used in conjunction with the Cambridge University Radio

Telescope until 1981 when it was moved to Duxford for display.

The Giant Würzburg is located west of Hangar 5 between the 1940s 'prefab' and the V1 ramp.

FLYING AT DUXFORD

As a complement to its static displays Duxford has a fine and active airfield, little changed from the days when it belonged to the Royal Air Force.

Flying takes place at Duxford throughout the year and the airfield is open to visitors at weekends during the winter months and daily between March and October.

During these hours, a small team of professional air traffic control personnel, working from the Second World War control tower, provide a Flight Information Service to

Preservation Ltd), and the Boeing **B-25 Mitchell** of The Fighter Collection are matched by the fighters of the Old Flying Machine Company (OFMC) and The Fighter Collection such as **P-51 Mustangs**, **Spitfires**, **Hurricane**, **P-40** and **P-38 Lightning**. Maritime types include the **Catalina** of Plane Sailing Limited,

▼ This P-47 Thunderbolt, owned by the Fighter Collection, carries the markings of the US 78th Fighter Group, based at Duxford between 1943 and 1945.
Mike Shreeve

▲ The T-33 of the Old Flying Machine Company.
John Dibbs

◀ Duxford's resident Bf109G.
Patrick Bunce

Duxford-based aircraft, pleasure flights and aircraft bringing visitors to the Museum.

A constantly changing collection of airworthy historic military aircraft is based at Duxford. Bombers like the Boeing **B-17 Flying Fortress** 'Sally-B', star of the film *Memphis Belle* (operated by B-17

▶ The Curtiss P-40M Kittyhawk of The Fighter Collection sporting the colours of 112 Squadron RAF, Western Desert 1943.
John Dibbs

the **Bearcat**, **Hellcat** and **Corsair** of The Fighter Collection and **Fury** and **Corsair** of OFMC. The Luftwaffe is represented by two German Second World War fighters, a Spanish-built **Messerschmitt Bf109J** (OFMC) and the **Bf109G** owned by the Ministry of Defence and operated by the Imperial War Museum. This is the only German combat aircraft still flying anywhere in the world that actually saw wartime action.

◀ Consolidated Catalina owned by Plane Sailing Air Displays and supported by the Catalina Society.
IWM Neg No. DUX(T)88/43/32

◆ Old Flying Machine Company Spitfire as the sun goes down at Duxford.
Jim Cooper

▲ B-17 Flying Fortress 'Sally-B' owned and operated by B-17 Preservation Ltd.
IWM Neg. No. DUX(T)88/45/29

Lighter military types are not forgotten, with the Second World War **Storch** and more modern **Chipmunk** of the Aircraft Restoration Company. These two aircraft have recently been joined by the newly restored **Blenheim** night fighter.

All these aircraft are maintained in flying condition, and may well be seen being put through their paces in demonstration flights at Duxford during the summer. Other historic and vintage aircraft frequently use Duxford, adding to the variety of interesting aircraft that may be seen flying here.

Duxford's airfield is ideally sited for staging air shows and each year several

special events are held, such as the Classic Fighter Air Show and the Duxford September Air Show. Duxford-based aircraft play a full part in these three-hour flying displays and at some events are joined by current military

▲ The Beech 18 (top) and Harvard of the Aircraft Restoration Company.
John Dibbs

▲ This Hawker Hurricane, operated by The Fighter Collection, was built in Canada during 1943. It carries the colours of No 71 'Eagle' Squadron RAF.
Cliff Knox

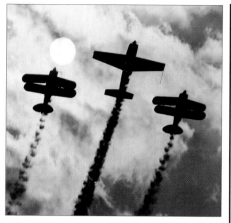

◀Duxford's air shows are among the best in Europe.
Cliff Knox

aircraft of the British and American armed forces, complemented by civilian display teams and solo aerobatic performers. These special events, which are often combined with ground displays, provide all the colour, pageantry, variety and excitement expected of modern events, and truly represent 'history in flight'. An integral part of flying activities at Duxford is pleasure flying, and flights around Duxford in a de Havilland Rapide or a more modern light aircraft are available (weather permitting) on Sundays throughout the year, and on Saturdays, Sundays and Bank Holidays as well as during school holidays in summer.

NOT TO BE MISSED...

At the end of the war in Europe in May 1945, Britain was faced with an immediate need for 1¼ million new houses. During the war almost half a million houses had been destroyed by bombs, or by V2 rocket attacks. As an emergency measure the Housing (Temporary Accommodation) Act, passed in October 1944, authorised the Government to spend up to £150 million on the provision of temporary prefabricated houses.

Up to January 1948 over 150,000 'prefabs' had been allocated at a cost of nearly £216 million, an average cost of £1,300 per unit. Although designed as temporary accommodation, 'prefabs' proved very popular with their tenants and many are still lived in today.

The Uni-Seco Bungalow was one of the most common types supplied. This particular bungalow was built in south London shortly after the war and was occupied until 1978 when it was purchased by the Museum from the Greater London Council and re-erected at Duxford. The bungalow, consisting of

a living room, two bedrooms, kitchen and a separate bathroom and W.C., has been refurbished to represent a 'prefab' at the time of Christmas 1946.

The photograph to the right shows the kitchen of the Duxford 'prefab' complete with appropriate crockery and cooking equipment.

The 'prefab' is located west of Hangar 5 between the Gibraltar Gun and the Giant Würzburg radar.

The Duxford Aviation Society, formed in 1975, is the largest and most active group of its kind in Britain. Its aims are to acquire, preserve and display British civil aircraft and to work closely with the Imperial War Museum towards the development of Duxford and its collections.

Since its formation the Society has built up an impressive collection of British airliners with the help of British Airways, Dan-Air, Monarch Airlines and Air UK.

Dan-Air have generously donated three of the airliners in the Society's collection. The **Avro York** was developed in parallel to the **Lancaster** and had the same wings, power plants, tail unit and undercarriage as the famous bomber. Although most Yorks were built for the RAF, many were sold to civil operators throughout the world and the British Overseas Airways Corporation operated them until 1957. During its career the York on display at Duxford flew the equivalent of 99 times around the world. In 1952 British European Airways became the first airline to operate the **Airspeed Ambassador**. By 1958 BEA Ambassadors had carried over 2.5 million passengers on European routes. The **de Havilland Comet 4** was the most successful version of the world's first jet airliner. In October 1958 the Society's Comet 4 made history when it became the first jet aircraft to

cross the Atlantic with fare-paying passengers on board. This historic aircraft was withdrawn from service in 1973 and flew into Duxford in February 1974.

The **Vickers Viscount** was the first turboprop aircraft to carry commercial passengers and the first British airliner to achieve substantial sales in North America. When production ceased in 1964 a total of 444 Viscounts had been built and over sixty airlines operated the type into the 1970s.

One of our most popular exhibits is the **British Aircraft Corporation/Aerospatiale Concorde**. Duxford's Concorde, number 101, was the third to be built for test purposes before the world's first supersonic airliner went into production. The French and British

prototypes made their maiden flights in March and April 1969. Concorde entered commercial service in January 1976 with British Airways and Air France.

The Society also displays a **Bristol Britannia**, **BAC Super VC10**, **de Havilland Dove**, **Handley Page Herald**, **Hawker Siddeley Trident**, **BAC 111** and a **Handley Page Hermes** fuselage.

The Duxford Aviation Society is closely involved in the conservation, restoration and maintenance of the collections at Duxford, working alongside the Museum's own technical staff. Special skills and experience are not necessary to become a member of the Society as there are rewarding projects available to suit all abilities and backgrounds. For membership details call at the Society's offices at the airfield or contact:

The Registrar
Duxford Aviation Society
Duxford Airfield, Cambridge CB2 4QR

▼ The Duxford Aviation Society's Concorde first took to the air in December 1971 and carried twelve tons of special equipment for four years intensive flight testing. In 1974 the aircraft flew from Britain to the east coast of America in 2 hours 56 minutes, then the fastest civil transatlantic flight. In August 1977 101 flew into Duxford and in its first ten years on display over 2 million people explored the interior of this revolutionary aircraft.
Jarrold

◀ Viscount 701, G-ALWF, entered BEA service in 1953 and is the oldest surviving Viscount in the world. It was sold to Channel Airways in 1964 and later served with Cambrian Airways, making its final flight in 1971. It was preserved at Liverpool until 1976 when it was dismantled and moved by road to Duxford, where it has been completely restored by Duxford Aviation Society members.
IWM Neg No. DXP(T)88/10/24

◀On the flightdeck of Concorde 101.
Reeve Photography

One of the newest attractions at Duxford is the Land Warfare Hall situated at the western end of the site. The purpose-designed building houses Duxford's impressive collections of tanks, trucks and artillery dating from the First World War to the Gulf War.

From the duckboards of the First World War a British rail head with a 1917 **Simplex Rail Tractor** can be seen. Nearby is a veteran of much action on the Western Front, the **4.5inch Howitzer**, and German equipment including the mighty **21cm Heavy Howitzer** and **7.6cm Trench Mortar**.

The inter-war period is represented by the tiny **Vickers MkVI** light tank. The British Army went to war in 1939 in machines such as these.

By 1940 the Germans were masters of Europe. Britain had hastily to improve its defence – witness the **Standard Beaverette** light patrol car and the **3.7inch Anti-Aircraft Gun** in its emplacement.

After three years of battles, British and Commonwealth forces drove the Germans and Italians out of North Africa. A mine-strewn desert tableau features a British **Valentine MkIII** tank guarding the passage of 'soft skin' transport.

▼ The 5.5" medium gun was the standard equipment of British medium artillery regiments for over 30 years. This is a camouflaged 5.5" making ready for action in Italy, 1943.
IWM Neg No. TR1402

▼ The First World War. The fixed 9.45inch heavy trench mortar (foreground) is flanked by (left) the British 4.5inch Howitzer and the US M17 75mm field gun. To the rear is the Simplex rail tractor and the German 21cm siege howitzer.
Reeve Photography

The Allies pressed on into Italy in 1943. It was a war of infantry and artillery, illustrated by the British **25-pounder Field Gun**, **5.5inch Medium Gun** and **7.2inch Heavy Gun**, impounded Italian guns and the long-serving German **10.5cm Field Howitzer** and **15cm Infantry Gun** which are all displayed.

A self-propelled gun is essentially a field gun mounted on a tank chassis. This gives greater mobility than a towed artillery piece especially in difficult terrain. The picture shows a Sexton self-propelled gun bombarding German positions in Italy in 1944.
IWM Neg No. NA20334

The Second World War - Eastern Front 1941–45. The German 10.5cm self-propelled gun, the Waffentrager.
Reeve Photography

▲ The Museum's Loyd Carrier was one of the last built and was once owned by its designer, Major V Loyd. The photograph shows a Loyd of an anti-tank unit in Normandy in 1944.
IWM Neg No. B8306

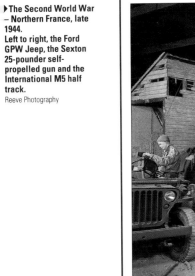

▶ The Second World War – Northern France, late 1944.
Left to right, the Ford GPW Jeep, the Sexton 25-pounder self-propelled gun and the International M5 half track.
Reeve Photography

▲ A menacing view of Duxford's Conqueror tank.
IWM Neg No. DXP(T)87/73/7

21

The titanic struggle between Germany and the Soviet Union on the Eastern Front from 1941 to 1945 is brought to mind with a scene from the war's closing stages. Soviet tanks, typified by the outstanding **T34/85**, engage in vicious urban fighting against fanatical German resistance.

The Western Allies' campaign through North-West Europe from June 1944 to May 1945 is represented by some of the hundreds of vehicle types used, from the amphibious **GMC DUKW** to the ubiquitous **Jeep** and **Sherman** tank. The three Headquarters Caravans of British Field Marshal Bernard Montgomery are also displayed here.

The post-Second World War period has

▲ The interior of the Leyland Caravan used by Field Marshal Montgomery as his office.
Reeve Photography

◀The Gulf War. Based on the Russian T54/55, the T69/2 is an updated Chinese-built copy.
Reeve Photography

◀British Army of the Rhine, 1946–1990. The Centurion Mk12 OP tank in a re-created German forest scene.
Reeve Photography

This Ferret Mk 2 Scout car was photographed in front of the Duxford Officers' Mess. It has been refurbished in the United Nations colour scheme in which it served with British Forces in Cyprus.
IWM Neg No. DXP(T)88/35/9

main British battle tanks, the ill-starred **Conqueror**, the ever changing **Centurion** and the **Chieftain**, are all on view.

At the end of the exhibition are vehicles from the recent past, the **Volvo Snow-cat** used in the Falklands in 1982, and a Chinese-built **T69** tank and a Soviet **BMP-1** armoured personnel carrier captured from Iraqi Forces in the Gulf War of 1991.

▼ 9.2inch guns were Britain's premier coastal defence weapon throughout the first half of this century. This gun, the largest artillery piece at Duxford, can be seen with two associated exhibitions close to Hangar 5.
Reeve Photography

been a time of smaller wars and operations that have involved British troops around the world. The US **155mm self-propelled gun** served in Korea, the mighty **Antar** tank transporter and **Centurion** tank in Libya and in Egypt at the time of Suez, the **Saladin** armoured car in the Far East, and the **Humber Pig** in Cyprus.

Britain's biggest military contribution in the post-war period by far has been to the British Army of the Rhine. The era's three

NOT TO BE MISSED...

Visitors to Duxford can experience the latest simulator technology in the Showscan® Dynamic Motion Theatre. Located in Hangar 1, the theatre has thirty-four seats arranged on two hydraulic motion platforms of seventeen seats each. The picture is projected by a patented Showscan® system which shows 70mm film at 60 frames per second onto a giant screen, linked to a sound system that fills the whole theatre. The image, sound and motion are all synchronised by sophisticated software to give the sense of taking part in the action. The ride takes about five minutes and there are regular shows throughout each day, usually with a choice of two films.

The *Battle of Britain Dogfight* was specially commissioned by the Imperial War Museum and features a Messerschmitt and Spitfires based at Duxford. Shot over the white cliffs of Dover, the film gives a spectacular pilot's eye view.

***Space Race* is on special release from America. It is an animated film about a space shuttle that wanders off course via a black hole and ends up in a galactic stock-car race. Fast, exciting and highly compulsive, *Space Race* will be available until at least May 1995.**

Duxford based Spitfire and Me109 which featured in one of the films shot specially for the Dynamic Motion Theatre.

John M. Dibbs

Duxford's very special links with the United States are reflected in its outstanding collection of American military aircraft of the Second World War and after – a collection which is the finest and most comprehensive outside the United States.

Several of the Second World War aircraft displayed at Duxford today have particular associations with the airfield. The **P-47 Thunderbolt** was flown by the US 8th Air Force 78th Fighter Group from Duxford during 1943 and 1944. Nicknamed 'The Jug', it was limited in range but very robust and especially suitable for strafing. During the final months of the war the 78th relinquished their Thunderbolts – it was said reluctantly – in favour of the **P-51 Mustang**, an aircraft considerably superior in terms of speed and endurance. The Mustang, described as possibly the best all-purpose fighter aircraft of the Second World War, had a range of up to 950 miles, enabling it to escort heavy bombers to and from raids deep into Europe. Its speed and manoeuvrability and its subsequent use in an offensive capacity, notably against enemy aircraft on the ground, was to contribute greatly to the growing Allied superiority over the Luftwaffe fighters by the spring of 1944.

The bombers which the fighters escorted are represented by 'Mary Alice', a Boeing

B-17 Flying Fortress. Flown operationally for the first time in 1941, the Flying Fortress became the mainstay of the US 8th Air Force's daylight bombing campaign. The Flying Fortress was described as an exceptionally stable aircraft, enabling pilots

▲ Upper picture
A P-47 Thunderbolt of the 82nd Fighter Squadron, USAF, with the 78th Fighter Group marking of black and white check cowling.
IWM Neg No. HU31375

▲ Lower picture
'Big Beautiful Doll', the P-51 Mustang of Colonel J D Landers who commanded the 78th Fighter Group from February to July 1945.
IWM Neg No. HU48197

▼ **Duxford's two resident B-17s photographed with the visiting G-FORT, 1987.**
IWM Neg No. DUX(T)87/27/14

to fly in close formation, and was notably strong – as proved by the number which limped back to their East Anglian bases despite appalling damage. Duxford is also the base for an airworthy B-17, 'Sally-B', which is flown frequently in the airfield's flying displays, an evocative sight for those who can recall the enormous bomber formations of the later years of the Second World War.

Another famous aircraft, the **Douglas C-47** or Dakota, was used for transport and for carrying troops. Dakotas remain in service in civil and military capacities to this day. The Museum's example saw service with the United States 9th Air Force in the Second World War.

The wartime US Navy is represented by a Grumman **Avenger** torpedo bomber. Avengers also served with the Royal Navy Fleet Air Arm from 1943.

The Museum's Boeing **B-29 Superfortress** is the only example displayed in Europe. The most advanced bomber of the Second World War, the B-29 played a vital part in the war

in the Pacific and was the aircraft which dropped the atomic bombs on Hiroshima and Nagasaki. The B-29 displayed at Duxford is a veteran of the Korean War. Nicknamed 'Hawg Wild' by the original crew who came from Arkansas, Duxford's aircraft was presented to the Imperial War Museum by the United States Navy in May 1979. It flew into Duxford the following year after an epic journey via Newfoundland, Greenland and Iceland.

Overshadowing the earlier aircraft is the enormous Boeing **B-52 Stratofortress**. This

B-52 saw service in the Vietnam War. The largest aircraft ever to land at Duxford, it flew in to join the collection in 1983.

The world's first supersonic combat aircraft was the North American **F-100 Super Sabre**. The type served with the US Air Force from 1954 and was extensively used in the Vietnam War.

In 1991 the last airworthy McDonnell Douglas **F-4J Phantom** flew into Duxford to join the collection. Duxford's F-4 saw action in the Vietnam War with the US Navy and went on to serve with the RAF. The versatile Phantom is one of the most successful aircraft designs of all time. Other recent

◄ **USAAF C-47s lined up in readiness for the Allied Airborne Army parachute drop in Holland, 1944. The Museum's C-47 took part in the famous Operation Market Garden' at Arnhem.** IWM Neg No. EA44036

▲ **The Museum's B-52 about to land at Duxford. B-52D, 56-0689, was handed over to the United States Air Force in October 1957. In common with all aircraft of the model it was converted to carry a conventional bomb-load of 60,000 lbs for service during the Vietnam War in which it flew some 200 missions. Its last posting was to the 7th Bombardment Wing of the US 8th Air Force at Carswell Air Force Base in Texas in October 1982. It was then donated to the RAF by the USAF and placed in the care of the Imperial War Museum at Duxford in October 1983.** IWM Neg No. 83/42/30

◄ **Duxford's B-29A, nicknamed 'Hawg Wild', entered USAAF service in May 1945.** Jarrold

acquisitions include a **Fairchild A-10 Thunderbolt II**, a **General Dynamics F-111** and a **Lockheed U-2** high attitude reconnaissance aircraft. All three types were used extensively during the Gulf War.

Not surprisingly, Duxford attracts many transatlantic visitors, among them United States servicemen currently stationed in Britain and Europe and war veterans who were based in England. More than two million US servicemen came to the United Kingdom during the Second World War, many of them based in East Anglia. Special exhibitions in

▼ **An A10 Thunderbolt II.**
United States Air Force

▲ **A Lockheed U-2.**
United States Air Force

Hangar 3 honour the United States 8th and 9th Air Forces. The 8th Air Force display, mounted with the support of the 8th Air Force Memorial Museum Foundation, uses maps, photographs, equipment and uniforms to tell the story of 'The Mighty Eighth'. Nearby is an exhibition of the insignia of the 8th Air Force. These are the motifs displayed by many squadrons as 'patches', on flying jackets, on signs and unit stationery. The particular designs chosen have a highly individual character, in many cases with a touch of Walt Disney. This colourful display attracts considerable attention.

A special Anglo-American exhibition, *Wings Across the Atlantic* is sited on the balcony of Hangar 1. Highlighting Anglo-American co-operation in aviation and the history of transatlantic flight, it has been generously sponsored by American Airlines.

▲ **Duxford's Phantom pictured in 1979/80 during its US Navy Service.**
Flying Colours via Mike France

▼ **The 8th Air Force Insignia Exhibition in Hangar 3.**
Photographic Assignments Limite

Duxford's links with the United States make it the perfect location for the planned **American Air Museum in Britain**. This ambitious development will stand as a memorial to the 500,000 American airmen who served from bases in Great Britain during the Second World War, some 30,000 of whom gave their lives. It will demonstrate the far reaching contribution United States Air Forces made to the Allied victory in 1945, with a section on the Gulf Campaign to bring the story of RAF–USAF co-operation up to date.

The separate building within the present Duxford complex has been designed by Sir Norman Foster. The dramatic 70,000 square feet structure will house the B-52 donated by the USAF and all the other important American aircraft at Duxford.

This building will cost £7 million, of which $7 million will be raised in the United States. A fund raising campaign is under way under the joint chairmanship of Marshal of the Royal Air Force Sir John Grandy and Mr Charlton Heston. His Royal Highness The Duke of Kent is Patron of the appeal.

How you can help

Please send your donation to **American Air Museum Office, Imperial War Museum, Duxford Airfield, Cambridge CB2 4QR**.

Sterling contributions should be paid to the Imperial War Museum Trust (American Air Museum Appeal). The Imperial War Museum Trust is a registered charity, No. L/244774/2.

Dollar contributions should be paid to the American Air Museum in Britain, a US non-profit corporation. Dollar contributions are tax deductible under Section 501(c)(3) of the Internal Revenue Code.

NOT TO BE MISSED...

The *X-Craft* Exhibition tells the story of the development and use of midget submarines during the Second World War. X-craft (the British code name for midget submarines) were developed for attacks on specialist naval targets in difficult waters and this unusual exhibition features two of these fascinating vessels, *X-51* and the remains of *X-7*.

The attack on the German battleship *Tirpitz* was one of the most hazardous operations undertaken by midget submarines. The ship was lying in what the German Navy thought was an impenetrable position, heavily guarded and surrounded by torpedo nets. Of the six X-craft which took part in the operation only two actually reached their target. Their Commanders were both captured after the attack and the craft scuttled.

The assault by two tiny midget submarines with only a four man crew apiece on the giant 42,000 ton battleship has been described as one of the most courageous acts of all time and both surviving Commanders were awarded the Victoria Cross.

The **X-Craft** Exhibition is located in Hangar 3.

A LIVING AND WORKING MUSEUM

▼ The large collection of airworthy historic aircraft on loan to the Museum is also the subject of maintenance work as each has to undergo a thorough annual inspection to ensure that it meets the exacting requirements of the Civil Aviation Authority. The Fighter Collection's Spitfire receives its yearly check.
Reeve Photography

The conservation and restoration of exhibits is one of the Museum's most important functions. Unlike the practice at many other museums, at Duxford this work is largely done in full view of our visitors, many of whom return to follow the progress of their favourite project.

Although this often extensive work provides a fascinating glimpse into the interior of an aircraft, Museum staff are frequently asked why it is all necessary. To answer this question, the visitor has to understand that aircraft are built from a wide variety of complex light-weight alloys, which although structurally strong, have little resistance to corrosion. This internal 'rusting', just like that on the family car, is why apparently complete aeroplanes have to be dismantled, the corrosion being treated before the structure and systems can be conserved.

In fact the term 'conservation' is a more accurate description of much of the work carried out at the Museum. Major restoration only becomes necessary when the aircraft has been acquired in a severely damaged, incomplete or badly corroded condition. This is also true of the Duxford Aviation Society's

▼ The suspension units of the Museum's Russian T34 tank being rebuilt.
Reeve Photography

▲ The Museum's technical staff are involved in the restoration and conservation of aircraft ranging from the First World War to those in service today, for example this Argentinian–built Pucara damaged during the Falklands Conflict.
Reeve Photography

◄ Members of the Duxford Aviation Society team at work on the Avro York which was donated to the Society by Dan-Air in 1986.
Reeve Photography

collection of civil aircraft, most of which have flown into the airfield for preservation.

Current aircraft projects include the painstaking rebuilding of the **Avro York**, one of only two left in existence, which is progressing well. The major reconstruction of a **Short Sunderland** flying boat is now complete but it will take a number of years to restore the exhibit internally to a standard representative of a service aircraft. An **Avro Lancaster**, which the Museum acquired in 1986, is also being returned to its wartime configuration.

One of the most exciting restorations to airworthy status at Duxford is the rebuilding of a unique **Hawker Sea Hurricane Mk 1**. This Canadian built example was converted in Britain for its Sea Hurricane role, complete with arrester hook, and was one of many which served with the Fleet Air Arm from 1941 to 1944. When it flies it will be the only airworthy example of a Sea Hurricane in the

◀ The interior of Duxford's Sunderland flying boat. ML 796 was last used as a café in Brittany, France and came to Duxford by road and sea in 1976.
IWM Neg No: DXP(T)87/64/3

◤ **Work progressing on the unique Sea Hurricane restoration project.**
Reeve Photography

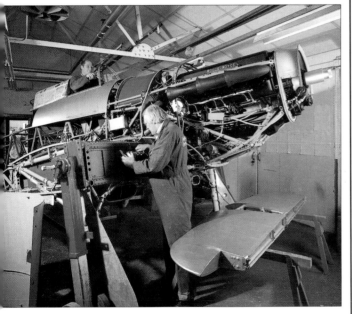

world. All these projects are being undertaken by different combinations of teams of Museum staff and skilled volunteers.

Many other exhibits are also the subject of restoration – vehicles, artillery, missiles and boats. The Museum has an active collecting policy and items on its acquisitions list turn up in the most unexpected places, frequently in a very sad condition. Often they have lain abandoned for years in farm out-buildings, scrapyards, British Army firing ranges and storage sheds. Several have been imported from abroad.

The restoration and conservation of these exhibits is undertaken by permanent staff, contractors and the Duxford Aviation Society Vehicle Wing. This work requires the same skill, care and patience as aircraft restoration, indeed the processes are very similar. The task is assessed, the original condition recorded, the paint carefully removed to reveal

▲ Lancaster MkX, KB 889, was built in Canada during 1944 and served with No. 428 Squadron (RCAF) at Middleton St George in 1945. After the war it returned to Canada and was modified for maritime patrol duties.
Reeve Photography

◀ Wherever possible Duxford's vehicles are restored to full working order. This engine has been completely refurbished before being returned to the Conqueror tank.
IWM Neg No. DXP(T)87/24/3

colour schemes and markings.

The restoration and conservation programme at Duxford is one of the largest operations of its kind in the world. Restoring such a large number of exhibits to top condition and keeping them that way represents an enormous challenge and makes constantly increasing demands on resources. Any individual or company willing to help by giving money, materials, or time is invited to contact the Conservation Manager on Cambridge (01223) 835000.

underlying colour schemes and markings (this is particularly important as vehicles and artillery pieces very rarely have log books to record their previous service history), damaged parts removed for repair or replacement, and corrosion treated. Most exhibits have parts missing or damaged beyond repair and replacement parts are sought. Scrapyards are often the most fruitful hunting grounds. Vehicle engines are overhauled and breech mechanisms on guns freed before re-assembly begins. Once this is completed the vehicles are painted in historically accurate, or appropriate,

NOT TO BE MISSED...

Visitors to Duxford can examine the only surviving example of a complete V1 launching ramp, from which German flying bombs were directed against London and southern England in 1944 and 1945. The first V1s were launched on 13 June 1944, a week after the Allied invasion of Europe. Though some 2,340 V1s caused considerable damage in London, Allied air supremacy meant that many of the V1s were shot down and their camouflaged launch ramps destroyed. Attacks on London diminished at the end of August 1944 as Allied forces moved across France and overran the V1 launching sites, but the 'doodlebugs' or 'buzz bombs' continued to fall on Britain until March 1945.

Duxford's exhibit comprises six sections bolted together to form a ramp 42m (nearly 140ft) long, angled at 6 degrees. The ramp at Duxford was salvaged from a Ministry of Defence range at Shoeburyness. Mounted on the ramp is an original V1 flying bomb on loan from the RAF Museum.

The V1 missile and launching ramp are located west of Hangar 5 next to the Giant Würzburg radar.

EDUCATIONAL SERVICES

Thousands of school children visit Duxford each year and their teachers find many different ways of applying the resources here to a wide variety of subjects at both primary and secondary levels.

The Education Service helps teachers and students to make the most of their visit to the

Museum. Many teachers take advantage of free preliminary visits and teachers' packs to plan their trips. The pack outlines the services available to schools and gives details of the reduced admission rates for pre-booked educational parties. All additional services for schools are provided free of charge.

To promote the children's enjoyment of their visit, talks are available on a wide variety of topics, along with worksheets specifically designed to guide them around the Museum and its collections. In consultation with teachers, the education staff adapt talks to suit the needs of particular groups and help teachers to develop their own worksheets and teaching resources. Additional help can also be given to schools with their preliminary or follow-up project work. Many children write direct to the Museum for information and assistance with school and examination projects.

The education staff plan to develop the service offered to schools, and any comments or suggestions from teachers are most welcome. Teachers' packs and further details can be obtained from the Education Office.

◀ **School groups are often given talks in the Duxford hangars close to relevant exhibits.**
IWM Neg No. DUX88/48/18

BUSINESS OPPORTUNITIES, SHOPPING, RESTAURANT

Duxford Airfield is a popular venue for corporate hospitality. The Museum can provide a range of versatile settings to suit all requirements. Duxford's special event day hospitality marquees are famous for key client entertainment but we can offer exciting hospitality days throughout the year and our flexible approach enables us to accommodate the most unusual requirements.

The Duxford Officers' Mess Conference and Business Centre is now a highly successful venue. Built in 1935 for the RAF, it has been restored to its former elegant splendour and five rooms are available for hire. It is ideal for exhibitions and conferences and major companies regularly utilise the facilities. The Mess also hosts private functions such as wedding receptions and parties. Several acres of land to the rear of the Mess are also available for hire. For details, telephone (01223) 833686.

A contributory factor to the rapid growth of Duxford has been the financial and material support of individuals and companies. Within the Museum's activities there are excellent opportunities for sponsorship and we welcome all proposals for mutually beneficial projects.

With its unique atmosphere and period buildings, Duxford is in great demand as a location for film and photographic shoots and the airfield's open spaces have a versatility that is hard to match.

If you would like to discuss the use of Duxford's range of facilities please contact the Commercial Co-ordinator.

Shopping A wide range of souvenirs and gifts for all the family can be found at the Museum shop in Hangar 1, including books, postcards, posters, model kits, videos and educational

◀ The Museum Shop.
IWM Neg No. DXPCN 91/42/13

▼ The Officers' Mess prepared for a wedding reception.
IWM Neg No. DXP88/65/5

▶ The Interlude Restaurant.
IWM Neg No. DXPCN 91/53/2

resources. A full-colour mail order catalogue illustrating a selection of products is also available. For your free copy please write to:

Mail Order Department,
Imperial War Museum,
Duxford Airfield, Cambridge CB2 4QR
or telephone (01223) 835000 x 245
(24-hour answer phone)

Gifts and souvenirs are also available in the Duxford Aviation Society Concorde Shop.

Restaurant Duxford's Interlude Restaurant, situated between Hangars 1 and 2, is open daily. The licensed restaurant offers a choice of food from sandwiches to full hot meals. Hot and cold beverages are available too, all served in re-created 1930s' surroundings.

Published by the Imperial War Museum, Lambeth Road, London SE1 6HZ
© The Trustees of the Imperial War Museum 1989 and 1992. ISBN 0 901627 95 X
Reprinted 1994, 1995.
Written and compiled by Carol Mahon with contributions from Francis Crosby, David Fearon, David Lee, Sue Sharp and David Henchie.
Designed by Peter Dolton.
Design and production in association with Book Production Consultants, 25-27 High Street, Chesterton, Cambridge CB4 1ND
Printed in England by George Over Limited, Rugby

The Imperial War Museum Duxford is operated in conjunction with Cambridgeshire County Council and the Duxford Aviation Society.